Four PAWS
Rumble and Tumble Through
the Streets in St. Augustine

Written by Linda R. Beall
Co-author, Itty-Bitty
Illustrated by Linda M. Brandt

ISBN: 978-0-9759533-7-2

Published by
Legacies & Memories
St. Augustine, Florida

(888) 862-2754
www.LegaciesandMemoriesPublishing.com

CONTENTS

Chapter 1..11
Four PAWS Vacation in St. Augustine, Florida

Chapter 2..22
Fun or Trouble

Chapter 3..29
More Trouble

Chapter 4..36
Predicament

Chapter 5..42
Ponce Comes to the Rescue

Chapter 6..46
Disciplined for Mischievous Behavior

Chapter 7..50
Four PAWS are Still Loved and Forgiven

Chapter 8..53
Words of Wisdom from Miss Linda
and Mr. John

Introduction

Four PAWS are four little dogs: Jessie, Max, Itty-Bitty and Preston. They love taking adventures and especially enjoy going on vacation with Miss Linda and Mr. John. This book is all about their adventures in the oldest city in the United States, St. Augustine, Florida.

Find out what mischief Four PAWS get into when they encounter pirates and a pirate ship. And see what surprise animal comes to their rescue. Plus, see what lessons they learn during their rumble and tumble in the ancient city.

The year 2015 marks the 450th anniversary of the founding of the city. St. Augustine is built on history and discovery. It was built by artists, businessmen, soldiers, clergy, and outdoorsmen.

The founding of St. Augustine in 1565 and the 450th Commemorative Birthday in 2015 are years of discovery in the past as well as the present.

Dedication

This book is dedicated to several individuals:

Linda M. Brandt is my illustrator and special friend.
We make a great team together.
Thank you, my friend.

Deborah Long is my editor and "clean upper."
You made me so proud of this book that
I want you to edit my future books.

Finally, I want to thank Samantha O'Connor, my niece.
She always wanted me to write a chapter book.
After I wrote this book, I gave it to her to read and review.
She put it into chapters. So, thank you, Samantha.
You did a great job. I love you and your parents very much.

Four PAWS
Rumble and Tumble Through
the Streets in St. Augustine

Chapter 1
Four PAWS Vacation
in St. Augustine, Florida

Four PAWS are on their special winter vacation to the lovely city of St. Augustine, Florida, with their owners, Miss Linda and Mr. John.

Four PAWS are four little dogs who have lived together since they were small. They are more like brothers and sisters, because they have experienced fun and scary moments together. They love to play and share good times.

St. Augustine is a new adventure and Four PAWS want to explore the city.

Did you know St. Augustine is the oldest city in the United States?

One of the dogs is named Itty-Bitty and she thinks she is a Diva. She also is scrappy and sassy. Itty-Bitty wants to ask you two questions.

"What do you like about being part of a family?"
Is it important to you?
Itty-Bitty really wants to know.

Jessie is the leader of the pack. Jessie is a white dog with big brown eyes. Jessie stares, begs and always wants a biscuit.

Max is a red dog whose face and tail make him look like a fox. Max always follows Jessie. Max's favorite joy is taking a nap on Mr. John's lap.

Finally, there is Preston, a red, tan, and black dog who thinks he is a superman. Preston protects Jessie, Max, and Itty-Bitty, along with Miss Linda and Mr. John.

"Do you have someone in your family who protects you?" asks Itty-Bitty.

Itty-Bitty is very curious and wants to know all about you. Think about her question because Itty-Bitty wants to know the answer.

Miss Linda, Mr. John, and Four PAWS drive into St. Augustine where they are greeted by two Spanish soldiers who are holding huge swords and wearing heavy Spanish armor.

The Spanish explorers founded this city in the year of 1565 and that is 450 years ago.

Four PAWS are excited! The dogs wag their tails and bark at the soldiers. The soldiers just look straight ahead and they do not move or say a word.

Preston thinks this is strange, but pretends he is a soldier, too.

Itty-Bitty wonders why the soldiers are protecting the city of St.Augustine.

What is this all about?

Four PAWS often sit and bark at their owners when they are hungry or bored. But today they are jumping from the back seat of the car to the front and will not stay still.

The dogs want to know if they have arrived yet, and when the car is going to stop.

Mr. John tells them to sit and be quiet. Miss Linda tells them to relax and take a nap.

All four dogs listen and sit quietly.

Itty-Bitty sits like she is told, but she does not like that command at all.

From the front and the back seats of the car, Four PAWS, Miss Linda and Mr. John see the Bridge of Lions, horses, buggies, and the red and green trolleys with lots of people riding in them. They also see the St. Augustine bayfront with many pirates walking alongside the pirate ships docked in the water.

Miss Linda and Mr. John drive past the Fountain of Youth Archeological Park, ancient churches, Flagler College, St. George Street, the Anastasia Island Lighthouse, and St. Augustine Beach.

Then Miss Linda and Mr. John drive through St. Augustine to Lincolnville. This community shares an important piece of St. Augustine history. Dr. Martin Luther King, Jr. marched down the streets of St. Augustine during the Civil Rights Era in 1964. In 1997, a street, Dr. Martin Luther King Jr. Ave., was named in his honor. Today it has a Corner Market, Lincolnville Museum and Cultural Center.

There is so much to see and explore in St. Augustine for people and dogs!

Now Miss Linda and Mr. John are ready to park their car and tour St. Augustine by foot.

If you ever visit St. Augustine, the first place you will want to see is the Castillo de San Marcos fort.

The city was founded in 1565, but this fort was not started until 1672. It was built to protect the settlers from being attacked by pirates and has survived many years of bombardment by invaders from other lands.

The fort is built of coquina shells from the bottom of the sea. Coquina is a mix of tiny sea shells and sand that stick together like glue. These shells are strong and can absorb the shock from the cannon balls. That is why tourists can see cannon balls embedded in the fort walls today. This makes Castillo de San Marcos very special.

The fort has soldiers, cannons, and pirates. The soldiers fire the cannons every afternoon as part of a re-enactment.

Inside are many rooms that once were officers' bedrooms, kitchens, and dining rooms.

There were other rooms that served as barracks, schools, churches and jails.

The fort is a big and an exciting place to visit and is just the right place for dogs to rumble, tumble, and get into lots of trouble.

Chapter 2
Fun or Trouble

Four PAWS are tired of sitting in the car and are ready to investigate the big fort. They want to run, play, and bark and they jump quickly out of the car when it finally stops. Four PAWS know their owners will be angry, but they want to explore! Plus, they need to get out and run in the fresh air.

What Four PAWS don't know is that in the fort and in most of the shops there are signs posted about service animals.

A Service Dog is a type of assistance dog specially trained to help people who have disabilities such as visual difficulties, hearing impairment, seizures disorders, and more. Jessie, Max, Itty-Bitty, and Preston are not Service Dogs.

"Only Service Dogs Allowed"

The dogs run straight to the fort.

The guards try to stop them from getting inside but Four PAWS think the guards are playing a game with them.

The dogs like this game, especially Itty-Bitty. It is so much fun to run from the guards and play with her brothers and sisters. Itty-Bitty points the way.

The harder the guards try to catch them the more fun Four PAWS have. The dogs weave and dodge throughout the fort.

Four PAWS like this game, but it is time to move on, and Itty-Bitty leads the way.

Jessie, Max, Itty-Bitty, and Preston are panting and very thirsty. They need a drink from a bowl of water. They run to St. George and Aviles Street, where local vendors and merchants have their places of business.

Aviles Street used to be called Hospital Street because an actual military hospital was there.

It cared for the sick and injured. The name Hospital Street was changed in the early 1920s. It became Aviles Street and it is the oldest street in St. Augustine and United States of America!

There are many old cobblestone streets in St. Augustine as well as historic homes and places of business.

Four PAWS are happy that many merchants keep bowls of water outside their shops for animals to drink. What a GREAT IDEA! Water bowls quench the dogs' thirst.

Now refreshed, Four PAWS are ready to move on. The dogs visit a few more shops, but again many shops have signs that read, "Only Service Dogs Allowed".

They can't go into these shops and this makes Four PAWS even more curious. But they learn this rule is for all dogs. This makes Four PAWS feel much better. It is just a rule for dogs.

All of us have to live by the rules.

Itty Bitty has a question to ask you.

"Can you name a rule you do not like but, have to obey?"

You don't have to answer right now. There are many rules and there is not enough time to think of a good answer. You can discuss this with the people who protect you.

Golden Rule

do unto others as you would have them do unto you

Chapter 3
More Trouble

The dogs see all kinds of people, including men and women dressed in pirate costumes. When they get to the end of St. George Street, Four PAWS see a park. The dogs run to the park.

This park is called, "Plaza de la Constitucion" in Spanish; in English it means "Constitution Square". It is the oldest public park in the United States! There, each dog rests, plays, and barks with each other.

Four PAWS walk among the musicians, the craftsmen, and the artists who are playing music, selling jewelry, and creating paintings for the visitors. Today is a special day when town government officials allow the vendors to sell their goods.

Everybody is having fun in the winter sun.

All at once, Jessie, Max, Itty-Bitty and Preston start barking. Their barking is getting louder and louder. People are stopping on the sidewalk to see what is the matter.

There in the middle of the street is a horse and buggy. Four PAWS have never seen such an enormous animal up close.

The driver of the buggy is very tense and nervous! He is afraid the dogs will scare his horse.

This is dangerous for the horse, the driver and the tourists.

The dogs run from the buggy toward a pirate ship anchored on the St.Augustine bayfront.

Miss Linda and Mr. John see Four PAWS running down the street and yell for them to stop. But Itty-Bitty and Preston do not stop. However, Jessie knows she needs to go back to the car and stay. Max agrees with Jessie and both run back to wait for Miss Linda and Mr. John. They know they are in enough trouble for one day.

Itty-Bitty becomes the new leader of the pack.

Along with Preston, they scamper and run to the waterfront.

Remember, Itty-Bitty is a sassy and scrappy. She is little, but being little doesn't stop her from getting into trouble.

Itty-Bitty should have been named "Little Miss Mischief," but everyone loves her, especially Preston.

Preston is her superman dog and he will always try to protect her as he follows her down to the waterfront.

Chapter 4
Predicament

Itty-Bitty just wants to see a pirate and a pirate ship.

"What is the big deal?" thinks Itty-Bitty.

She and Preston continue walking along the St. Augustine bayfront where they see many boats and ships bobbing up and down in the water.

They abruptly stop when out of nowhere appears a sleek black pirate ship. It has two large crossbones on its sails. This vessel was made of whale and fish bones and it is rumored that a few human skeletons were added into the mix.

Itty-Bitty is excited and fearless. After all, she wants to see a pirate ship, but she does not expect to see a real pirate with a sword, pistol and whip guarding the ship.

Itty-Bitty and Preston are surprised to see a man dressed in black wearing a strangely shaped hat who has a peg leg and a patch over his left eye. Itty-Bitty tries to sneak on the ship. Preston follows along to protect her. The pirate orders Itty-Bitty and Preston to stop. They do not stop and the pirate chases them with his sword and whip. The dogs run up the gang-plank, then they stop and look down into the water. They are frightened by what they see.

What do you think they see?

Itty-Bitty and Preston look up and bark. The dogs bark again as the pirate comes closer with his sword and whip.

Itty-Bitty and Preston have nowhere to run but must jump off the gangplank into the water. They swim the doggy paddle away from the ship, and Itty-Bitty and Preston are getting very tired. They need a boat or a big fish to tow them to shore.

Whoever is going to help them better get there quickly. Itty-Bitty and Preston cannot remain afloat much longer.

Chapter 5
Ponce Comes to the Rescue

In the water, on the other side of the ship, Ponce de Dolphin is having fun.

He is snorkeling, diving and doing his dolphin kick close to the ship when he notices a lot of splashing and hears loud yelping.

Ponce pops his head out of the water and is surprised by what he sees. Ponce sees two little dogs struggling in the water.

Ponce de Dolphin knows he has to save Itty-Bitty and Preston and help them back to shore. So he gently swims underneath the dogs and Itty-Bitty and Preston climbed onto his back. It is slippery but each dog grabs a flipper with his front PAWS.

Ponce tows them to the land.

Itty-Bitty and Preston thank Ponce de Dolphin for saving their lives and promise never to set foot on a pirate ship in St. Augustine ever again, unless they receive permission from the captain of the ship.

Chapter 6
Disciplined for Mischievous Behavior

Itty-Bitty and Preston have had enough excitement for one day. They want to go back to the car. Both dogs are hungry, wet, and cold. They miss Jessie and Max. The dogs want to lick Miss Linda and Mr. John to tell them they are sorry they ran away and they are glad to be back where they belong. All they want to do is to take a long cozy nap in the back seat of the car.

Itty-Bitty and Preston are anxiously walking back to the car. Will Miss Linda and Mr. John be angry at them? What will they say? Will they be disciplined? Itty-Bitty does not care, she just wants to get back to the car and take a nap. Preston walks confidently alongside Itty-Bitty, but he knows they are in trouble. He worries about what is going to happen to him and to Itty-Bitty.

Finally all four dogs are reunited with Miss Linda and Mr. John. Yes, Miss Linda and Mr. John are upset with Itty-Bitty and Preston for running away. Miss Linda and Mr. John were worried about the missing dogs. Plus, Jessie and Max are not happy with Itty-Bitty and Preston either. They were worried, too. Everybody climbs back into the car and is very quiet. The dogs do not bark and Miss Linda and Mr. John do not smile or talk.

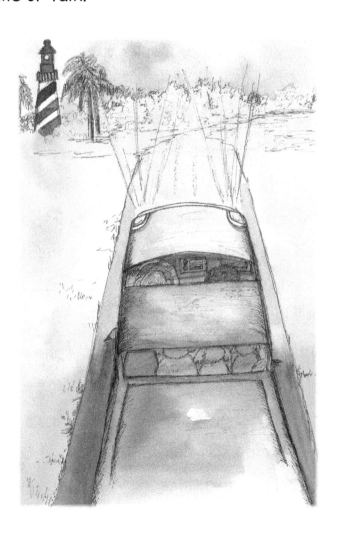

Chapter 7
Four PAWS are Still Loved and Forgiven

Later that day after a few hours of rest and being quiet, Four PAWS have their dog treats. Their favorite treats let them know that even though Jessie, Max, Itty-Bitty and Preston have been naughty, Miss Linda and Mr. John still love them and all is forgiven. Four PAWS know they have to behave the rest of the trip. The dogs stay in the car while Miss Linda and Mr. John tour the Alligator Farm, Flagler College, Casa Monica Hotel, and the Lightner Museum.

When Miss Linda and Mr. John return to the car, they discover Four PAWS sleeping contently in the back seat. The dogs are still tired from all the exciting adventures they have had in St. Augustine. Now it is time for Jessie, Max, Itty-Bitty, and Preston to take their own tours and have some exercise. St. Augustine is a pet friendly city and Four PAWS are allowed in the Fountain of Youth Park, on St. George Street, at the Oldest Wooden Schoolhouse, in the Colonial Quarter and on the grounds of Mission Nombre de Dios (The Cross). This makes the dogs very excited and happy.

They can run, play, and bark with each other some more.

If you have not been to these famous sites, you must visit them and you will be awed like Four PAWS, Miss Linda and Mr. John. Four PAWS also enjoy the restaurants with patio seating that allow them to eat and drink alongside of Miss Linda and Mr. John. Dinner is dog delicious. After dinner it is time for bed and that is not a problem in St. Augustine. They stay at a dog friendly hotel and Four PAWS sleep in comfort.

The next day, Miss Linda and Mr. John decide to tour many old and historic churches in the city, including the Cathedral Basilica of St. Augustine, Grace United Methodist Church, St. Augustine Memorial Presbyterian Church, St. Paul A.M.E. Church, Trinity Episcopal Parrish, and Ancient City Baptist Church. These are only a few of the many churches they toured and there is not enough time for more. Miss Linda and Mr. John end their vacation in St. Augustine by touring the Old St. John's County Jail and the Anastasia Island Lighthouse. When they return next year they plan to see new sites and revisit old favorites.

They like touring in the winter when the weather outside is cool. The temperature today is 55 degrees. It is a perfect season for dogs to rest in the car between tours. Now they are going home where they belong.

Chapter 8
Words of Wisdom from Miss Linda and Mr. John

In closing, always remember it is great to go on vacation and have fun.

When you are traveling with others, remember, vacation is just not about you and what you want to do. You must share choices with other people and dogs.

All four dogs in our story are different and yet they are the same. They love adventure and want a good life like you. But Itty-Bitty wants you to be safe in whatever you do.

Remember, the next anniversary of this beautiful city of St. Augustine is a special day. The year 2,015 marks 450 years since the city was born. In the year, 2,065 the city will celebrate 500 years of birthdays. Every year between 2,015 to 2,065 is special and unique.

Four PAWS are honored that you read their book and understand why St. Augustine is so important to the state of Florida and to the United States. This city has a lot to offer people and dogs. But take a tip from Itty-Bitty and Preston and watch out for pirates with swords, pistols, and whips.

Take a second tip from Jessie, Max, Itty-Bitty and Preston and obey the rules. Four PAWS care about you.

The End
By Linda R. Beall and Itty-Bitty

P.S. Itty-Bitty can't wait to write about the next adventure with Four PAWS, Miss Linda and Mr. John. Don't forget, Itty-Bitty has many questions to ask you.

The Author, Linda R. Beall

Linda R. Beall is the author and creator of the Four PAWS series. Four PAWS are four little dogs named Jessie, Max, Itty-Bitty, and Preston.

Her previous books include: Four PAWS and One Old Cat; We Four PAWS and Me at Yellowstone National Park; and Four PAWS and Lucky Little Duke Dog.

An underlying theme in all of the books is that we are all different and yet we are all the same. We want the same things in life regardless of who we are. Each book also includes several life messages.

Linda is the oldest of ten children. Growing up, she loved to tell stories, and any free time she had, she wrote and told more stories. After graduating from Salisbury University with a degree in Social Work and raising two sons, she and her husband John, moved to St. Augustine, Florida, and she once again spends her days writing stories and caring for several little dogs.

To learn more about her books or to contact her, visit www.LindaBeall.com.

The Illustrator, Linda M. Brandt

An award-winning artist, as well as author, Linda M. Brandt has been painting for most of her life. She illustrates her own books and several other authors' books.

While still in high school, Linda won three gold key awards and the Grumbacher award for her art. At nineteen, she began her career professionally as a political cartoonist. Later, she was commissioned by various groups and individuals to paint portraits of President Ronald Reagan, a governor and several senators. She has been at the creative helm of many large corporations, as well as WTLW-TV.

Her art is shown at the prestigious GNG Gallery in St. Augustine, Florida, and at www. yessy.com/brandt. She and her husband, Scott, live on Anastasia Island, Florida, with their Labradoodle, Max.

CPSIA information can be obtained at www.ICGtesting.com
Printed in the USA
LVOW02s1507030715

444628LV00007B/7/P

9 780975 953372